I am a dog.

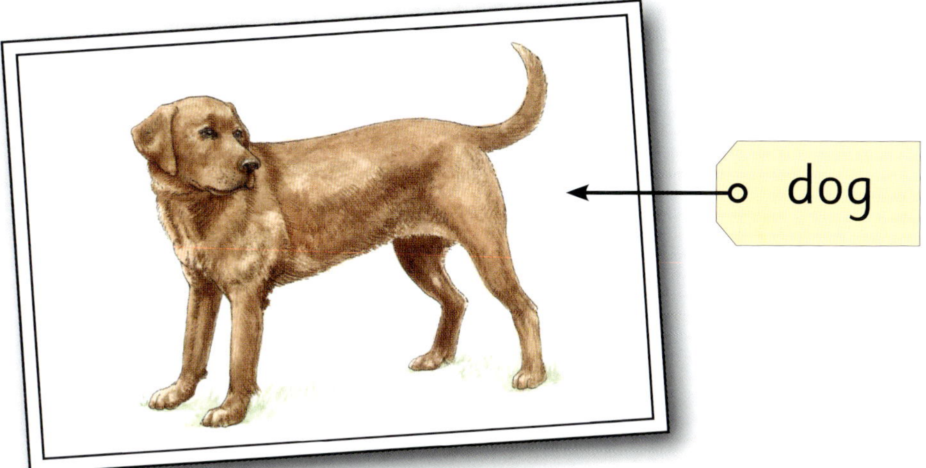

A dog has pups.

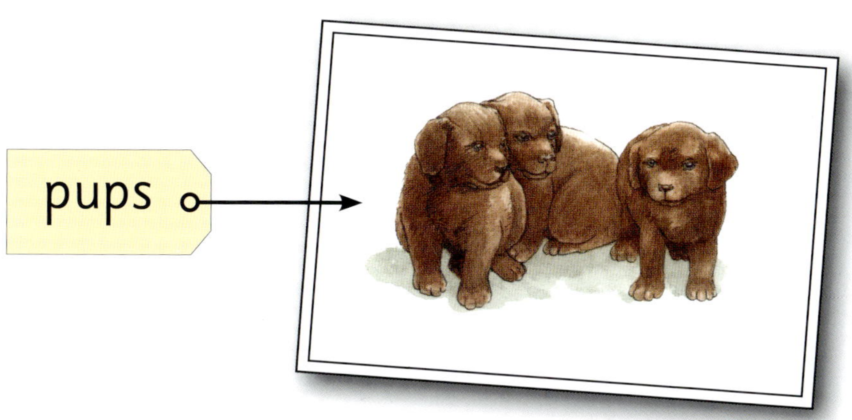

I am a goat.

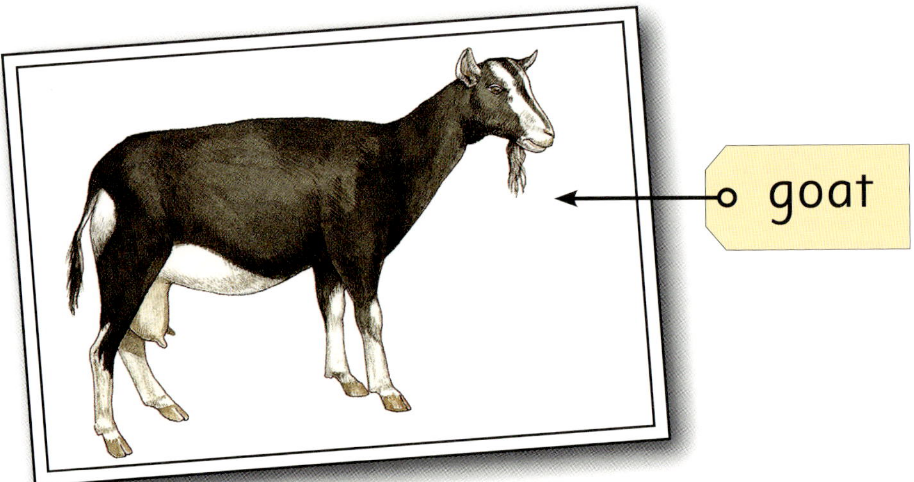

A goat has a kid.

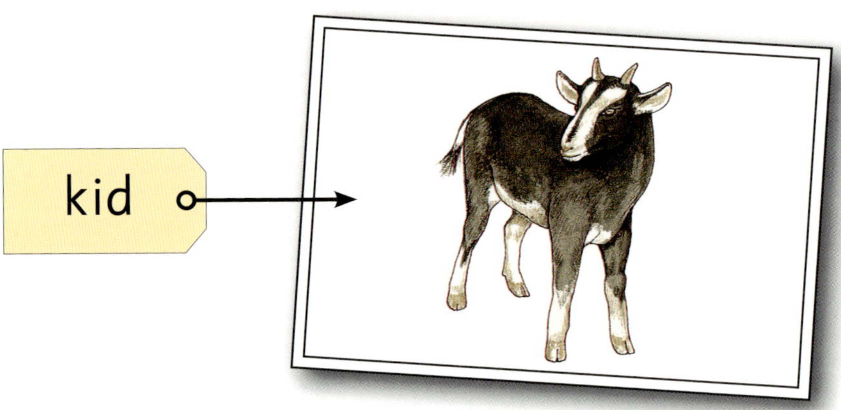

I am a horse.

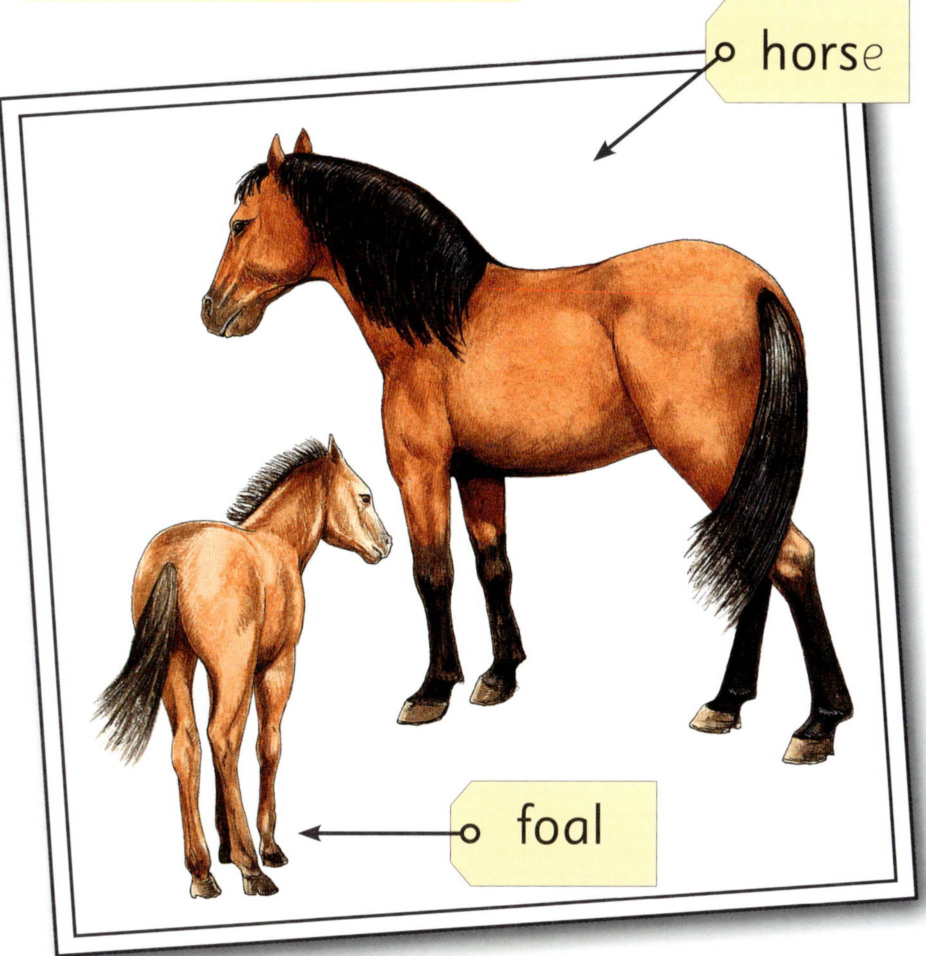

A horse has a foal.

I am a sheep.

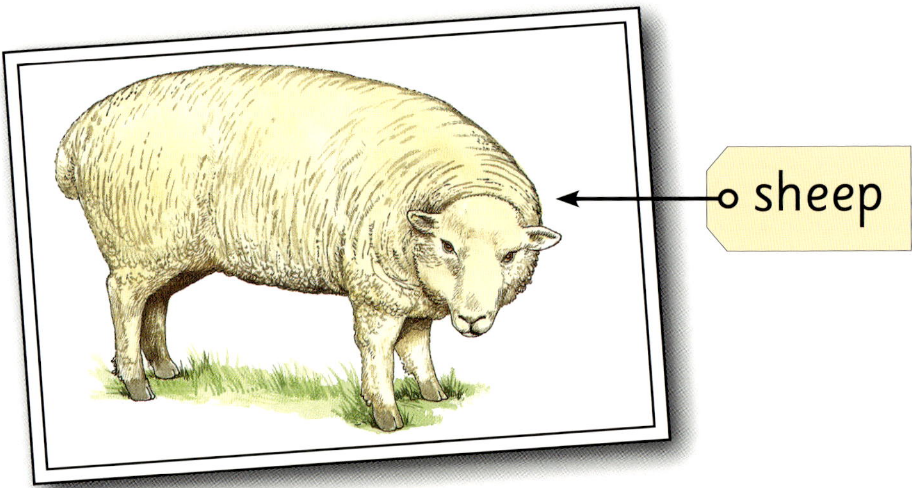

A sheep has a lamb.

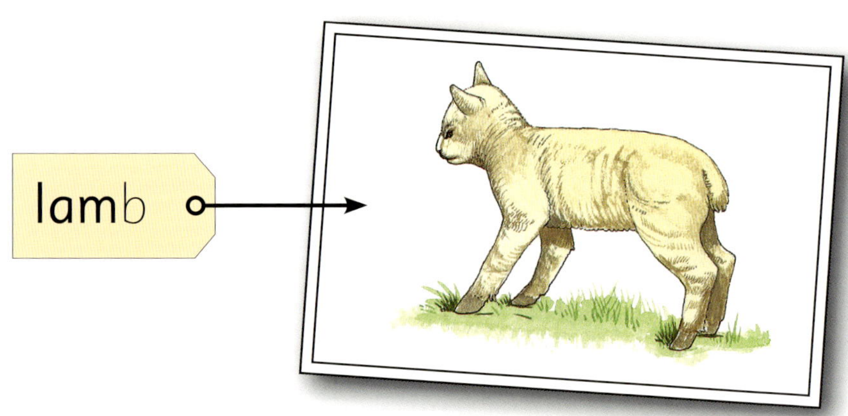

I am a cat.

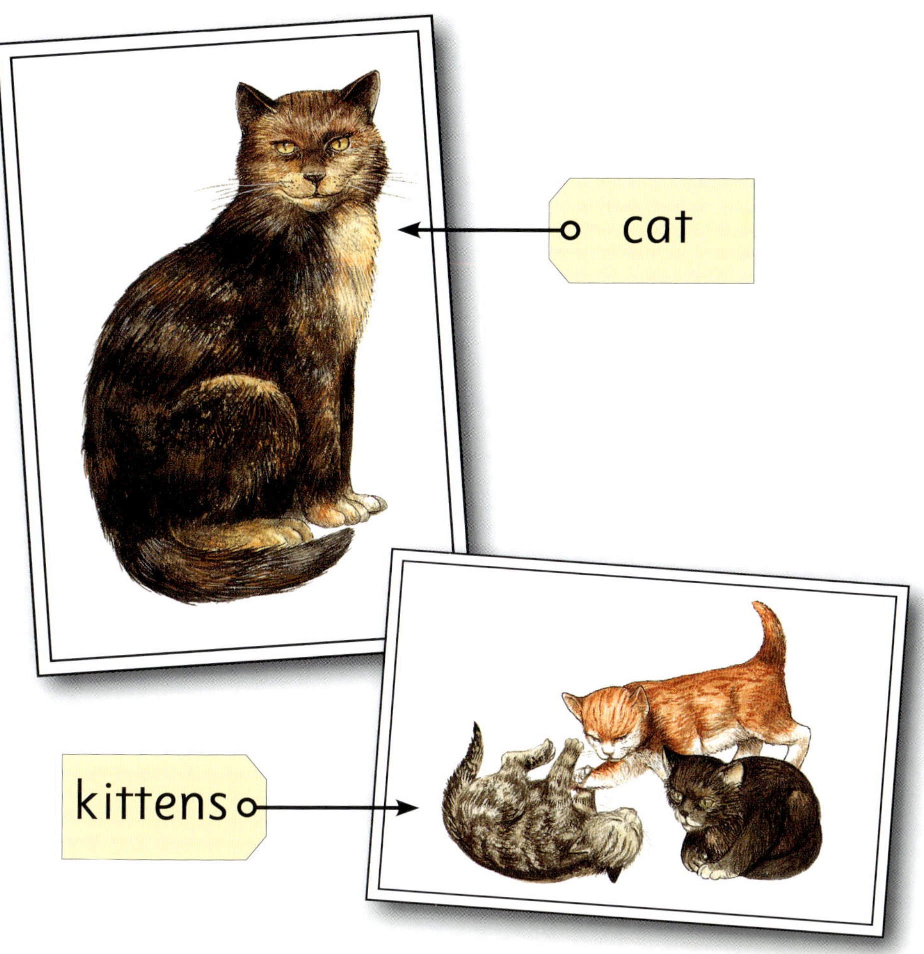

A cat has kittens.

I am a rabbit.

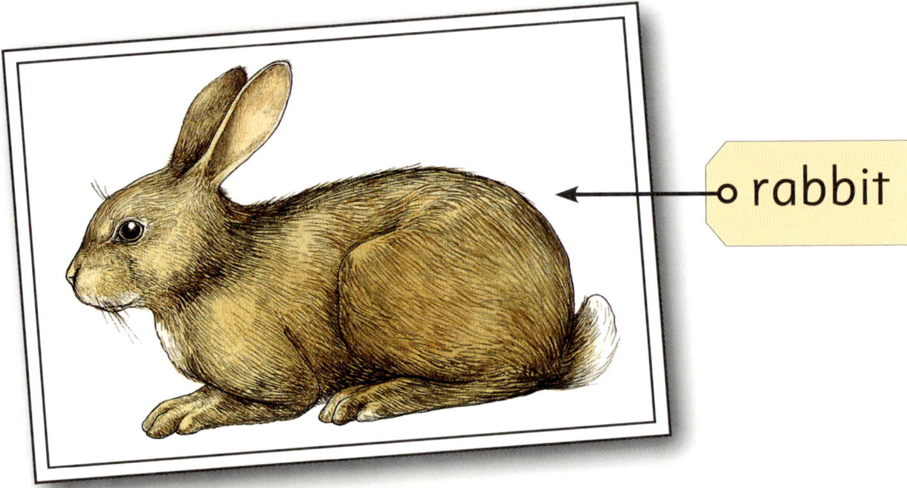

A rabbit has kittens too.

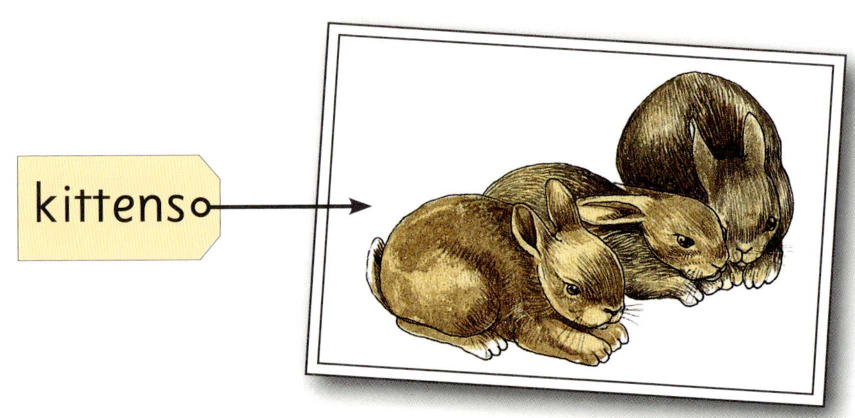

I am a hen.

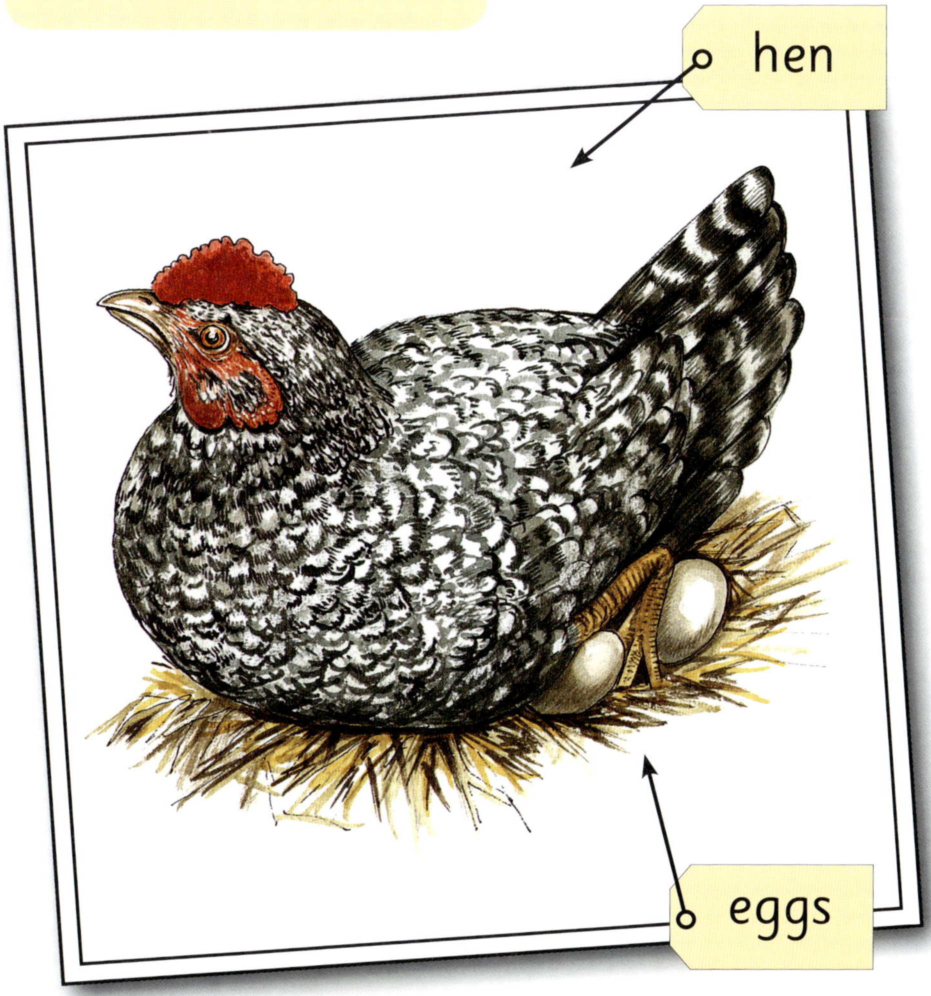

A hen has eggs...

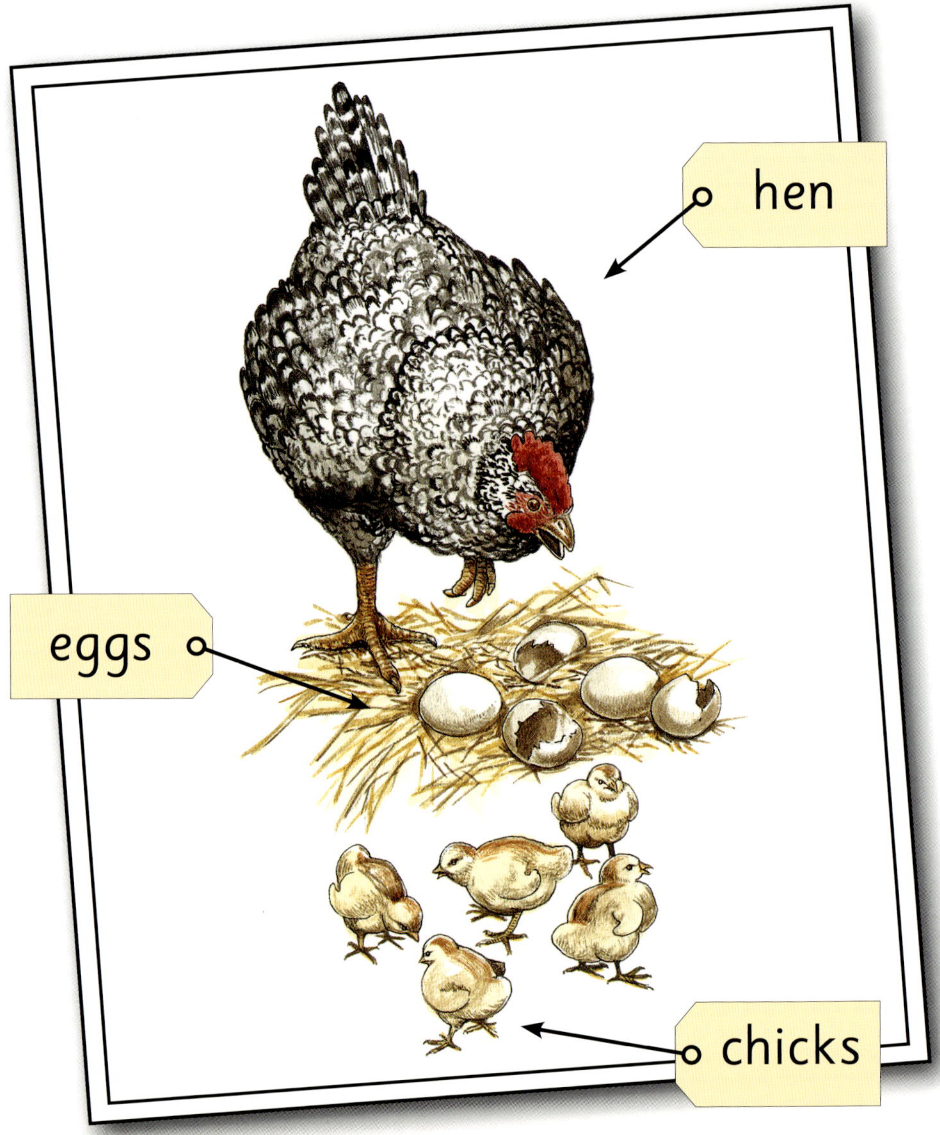

...that hatch into chicks!